LICORICE

LICORICE

poems

ELLEN C. BUSH

DURHAM, NORTH CAROLINA
2018

LICORICE

Copyright © 2006, 2018 by Ellen C. Bush

Grateful acknowledgement is given to the periodicals in which the poems in this volume first appeared. "Glue Skin" first appeared in *Puerto del Sol*. "Boy Running with Muffler and Tailpipe" first appeared in *Inch*.

Published in the United States of America

Library of Congress Cataloging-in-Publication Data

Bush, Ellen C.
Licorice: poems / by Ellen C. Bush
p.   cm.
softcover ISBN: 978-1-4951-7878-8
e-book ISBN-10: 0-9887044-4-7
e-book ISBN-13: 978-0-9887044-4-2

Cover design by Flying Hand Studio
Cover photograph by Stephen Grubb
Interior design by F. H. Spock and Associates

Published by
BULL CITY PRESS
"Hit bull, win steak."
1217 Odyssey Drive
Durham, NC 27713

www.BullCityPress.com

CONTENTS

TO SLEEP

Even with your eyes
open, you resemble
the dead. We watch TV,
not talking.
A man in a blizzard
kills a large beast
and slices across
its grounded belly.
He pulls out miles
of innards, staining the snow
red, and crawls inside.
It is warm.
He sleeps.

The movie over, you
remember me, touch my hair.
You have drunk yourself
into a pink warmth,
and your hand near
my icy cheek
reminds my skin
of its own absences:
color, heat.
Your hand falls
as you fall away
into sleep, all sense
sinking into the couched
bulk of your body.
I imagine the clean

knife in my hand guiding
itself along a line
under your shirt; the wound
opening before it thinks
to bleed; your sleep
a rosy envelope; and
my body, small, in it.

ALSO ACCIDENTAL

the way the surgeon lost count of the stitches
the way the skin grew back
the way one side of your face is stretched so tight
    it will never wrinkle
the way the other side will
the way you forget
the way one nugget of glass is sewn into your chin
the way the lump glides under the surface
the way it grinds when it presses against bone
the way you flinch
the way you guide someone's fingers to it
the way you stay still
the way that hand pulls back
the way that hand returns, thinking it is the first
    to touch you there

APPROACHING Y AXIS

Drawing away from the blue
light of your house, our breaths
cloud in the swelling dark. We are
separate heats in separate coats.
Walking closer and closer, our bodies
pull toward each other, toward
a singular warmth:
a heat we cannot achieve.
The pull, two curves
bending toward the same axis:
an infinite approach
to an impossible arrival.

BOY RUNNING WITH MUFFLER AND TAILPIPE

looking for a girl
whose only emergency
is automotive

SAME SONG, DIFFERENT VERSE

It's the dream where all your teeth fall out,
only this time you remember: this is

something you've awakened from and left behind
a dozen times already. What's happening to you
now, in a while, never happened.

It's an easy joke of losses, once you know
this nightmare's bluffing. Your tongue
takes it well, tears the inside of your mouth to pieces.
You spit teeth like watermelon seeds.

NEW GIRLFRIEND

I'm in the car with the new girlfriend
of someone I once wished was my lover.
In the dream the girlfriend is played by a bartender.
The lover plays himself but does not appear
in any scene; he exists now as he did
when I was nineteen: liquid, absent.
And she leans over and cries in my lap, she is crying
the song I used to know the words to.
She says the words and I say yes,
it's true, there is nothing you can do.
Inevitable, impossible—same thing, I don't say—
what can you expect? She is almost smiling.
Of course. She starts the engine again
and we drive a long time.

THE HANGED LEG

His body forgets.
Right Leg has lost memory of motion,
the lift-and-push of walking. It hangs
limp from the hip's noose.
Left Leg has forgotten something else—
a bullet, a woman, a reason for lingering.
It is still in the habit of getting out of things
like cars and mud and difficult rooms.
It weighs less, would dance if Right
Leg would let it. But they are one body,
his body, a tipped scale. He can no longer
imagine perfect balance or an even rhythm.
He pulls himself down roads of snow
making lines: pass, do not pass.

A COMFORT OF PLUMS

Where his body used to be:
her lip, purple bulb asleep
in a bowl of milk, face closed
against porch-rail stripes of light.
Her lip: what she licks smooth once in this sleep
with no witness but the large black ant,
sugar seeker, creeping from chair
to body, discovering plum,
feeding there.
Even when she flinches,
dreaming her own easy fist,
a sudden blow,
the insect holds on, holds
tight at the lip of her violet
comfort, where the flavor is quiet
every hour of her loud sleep.

THE GIRL IN HER

Never listens to anything but water, water
carrying sound and hushing it. On her haunches
by the creek, she bends her face down
to wait for what she said yesterday. When
something comes she laughs, whispers back,
I lied. It is always this funny, the way truth returns,
yesterday's mistake. Maybe she does it on purpose.
What she knows she does not say. That water is
the cooled version of blood, running away from itself
in a wet murmur. That the blue heat in her veins
is thickening in a confusion of facts. And that
balance is the most important thing as she hovers
over the water, burying her hands in the thin dirt
brown of her hair, lifting the length up to cool her neck.

NEW MUTE

They have cut out the cancer and,
        with it, your tongue. Dreaming,
do you taste burnt toast, bitter coffee?
Do you argue with the Presbyterian
        minister?

Awake, you learn to tend to your invalid wife
        with a new understanding,
as if you've finally joined her
in the wordless place
        where the stroke left her.

But the space in your mouth spreads fast.
        The house widens, waits for sounds
it recognizes: the rocking chair
creaking you back and forth,
        the telephone ringing on its hook.

Uncle! Close the doors, forget the old tease
        of tying my loose teeth to doorknobs.
Bring this house down to size
around the woman whose last name you gave
        and whose first name I took.
Save the kitchen, the living
room for the dying, and the dining room
        where you sleep lightly beside her.

PHOTOGRAPH

You were turning ghost already:
the summer before you
sank, a limp wreck,
to lake's bottom,
you stopped looking
the camera in the eye. Here,
six of us grinning on the dock
and you, in the back row,
face turned toward the water,
eyes dark circled blurs,
mouth open.
What palpable fact rose up
from the water and entered
your parted lips that time?
What turned you early?
I still try to find you
in that looking-away face:
in the look, in the away.

GLUE SKIN

The transparent sheets peeled from
your palms hang crisp. This is
what remains of you here: a collection
of hands thin as moth wings but less
like velvet. I unpin one, lift it
to the light, and it becomes the history
of you, every line exposed—heart, head, life,
fate. The lines cross, break, just
disappear. I unpin all your hands,
stacking them into my own palm.
The bottom layer warms against
my skin, softens at the mounts of Moon
and Venus. As I lie down, the pile tumbles
onto my shirt, one of your hands slipping into
my open collar, there where the pulse beats out
the rhythm of its heat. One hand remains
in mine, still stuck. I fumble at the buttons
of my shirt until it opens, then gather up
the scattered glue skins, lay them
against my own, neck to belly
prints fluttering, coming
to rest like moths at a pane of light, clinging.

MY GRANDMOTHER'S LEGS

I.

My aunt Rachel has them now. I never saw them young,
but Rachel in heels is still a sight,
         a sexy fifty-eight. Seeing her, I imagine

the tall version of my Grandmother,
         before a century's gravity
pulled her so many inches closer to my own height. The city legs
         she must've had once,
         to carry her from the Carrollton farm

to Atlanta: a downtown job, her name still her own,
         her dark dress just below the knee,
             a shiny black heel sloping into

a flash of calf: the last thing to see
         when the elevator's iron gate clicked
and the floor lifted up into the ceiling.

II.

Maybe there were fiddles, but the music
         came from the caller's
         wild instruction, the floor roaring
           under heavy feet,
the dancers' shouts.

Eight years old and shy,
I went one round with a man named Ham,
then sat in a folding metal chair with a sweaty Coke
and watched Grandmother and Granddaddy bow

and spin, arms locking and
                     unlocking, *swing-now, change-yr-partner*,
                  so fast,
      till the red gingham shirt
matched the red gingham dress again

to touch and pass on,
        their windy dance a thunderstorm,
        Grandmother's dress wheeling high and wide.

III.

        What surprises us all is that it isn't
a broken hip
or a slipped disk,
               but a lacerated face
          held together
          with string,
eyes blacked out,
white hair
        skunked with a stripe of dried blood
           from yesterday's highway

accident. When Rachel and I lift her
                    from the bed
                    she groans to shift the pile of broken sticks
            inside her chest.

She insists on wearing her slippers home, and I
lean into some cruel
                    fairy tale,
            forcing the size-eight shoe onto
the (now) size-ten foot,

her bare legs flexing scarless,

her survival pumping
            from those two wells,

swollen, whole.

FOLLY BEACH

Two fists full of secrets came whispering,
but the sea's licking up everything I ever held.
A voice from the speechless dark calls out
the rare syllables of my name.
Thinking I am water's first word,
I turn to the sand, frantic for a witness.
There in the blinding grays of night
a figure my hands would recognize
stands, a vertical extension of empty beach,
motionless and glowing white.
Hip deep in a swirl going flat and silent,
slow thighs pull toward shore.
For what is there to do but move
toward the thing that knows my name
and speaks it, out loud and out of reach.

CONVERGENCE OF THE TWINS

I am expecting her,
but I will be away
when she struts,
elegant pigeon,
right into my kitchen
to rearrange my pans and dishes,
to fill my pots
with angel hair
and leave them
foaming on the stove.
She will dismantle
my only clock,
draw obscene pictures in the dust
on my great-grandmother's
cherry dresser.
She will browse
through my two-car garage,
fondling everything
from Big Wheels to life jackets,
strolling over the oil spot,
tracking the black back
into my newly carpeted living room.
I will come home
to find her cooing
in my lover's arms.
Knowing I abandoned
my singing voice
long ago,
she will open her throat
and yodel me

right out of my own house:
down the street,
around the block,
her wild vowels
twisting around my ankles
and circling overhead.

SOMETIMES THE WEATHER

His ready sleep surprises her: what act
of weather could send him lazy into this?
When he entered the house wet she wondered what
he was coming in from, what dampness
happened. He can't explain it. Sometimes the weather
is everything. She goes looking for it
herself, cocks her head as if the horizon
needed righting. Then the sky: white
and vague as she holds her palms out to catch
the something falling out of the nothing.
Someone tell her it is yes, raining,
for this weather is as difficult
as sleep. Who can say what state this is,
or what white heart's blank precipitate?

BUTTERFLY

A butterfly, frantic. It doesn't know I am no flower. I am no flower. Butterfly, no sweet here. I fight for a while, swat and shoo it. Stubborn thing, it won't go. It plays, prickling along my arm. Let it. In my hair, fluttering in its tiny panic. Let it. Leaning forward, hair falls around my face, and butterfly is trapped now between hair and cheek, tickling there, humming there, and I am still but grinning. Let it. And then another butterfly appears. Now there are two. Let them. And it happens like this, that there is a man now on the porch to give witness to everything—and he is proof that I am awake, that the butterflies and I are not imagining. The man doesn't speak because of what is happening in my hair. He observes with the curiosity of a biologist, studying the behavior of the insects. I can smell him, he smells like soap and the tart citrus of the sweat that starts so early on August mornings.

HER MOUTH

Caught in the white light of chin and cheeks,
those lips, red as emergency,
circle the dark licorice pit of teeth and tongue.
That scarlet *o*, the siren against desire.
That black hole, the cave
each of us wants to crawl into.

ABOUT THE AUTHOR

PHOTO / LAURA McLEOD

ELLEN C. BUSH was born in Columbia, South Carolina. She earned a BA from the University of North Carolina and an MFA in creative writing from Cornell University. She now lives in Durham, North Carolina.

ALSO FROM BULL CITY PRESS